A DAY IN THE LIFE OF AN AFRICAN VILLAGE

Library of Congress Cataloging-in-Publication Data

Davidson, Avelyn.
  A day in the life of an African village / by Avelyn Davidson.
      p. cm. -- (Shockwave)
  Includes index.
  ISBN-10: 0-531-17748-3 (lib. bdg.)
  ISBN-13: 978-0-531-17748-8 (lib. bdg.)
  ISBN-10: 0-531-15545-5 (pbk.)
  ISBN-13: 978-0-531-15545-5 (pbk.)
  1. Africa--Social conditions--21st century--Juvenile literature. 2. Children--Africa--Social
conditions--Juvenile literature. 3. Africa--Rural conditions--Juvenile literature. I. Title. II. Series.

  HN773.5.D38 2008
  307.76'2096090511--dc22

2007018961

Published in 2008 by Children's Press, an imprint of Scholastic Inc.,
557 Broadway, New York, New York 10012
www.scholastic.com

SCHOLASTIC, CHILDREN'S PRESS, and associated logos are trademarks
and/or registered trademarks of Scholastic Inc.

08 09 10 11 12 13 14 15 16 17
10 9 8 7 6 5 4 3 2 1

Printed in China through Colorcraft Ltd., Hong Kong

Author: Avelyn Davidson
Educational Consultant: Ian Morrison
Designer: Juliet Hughes
Editor: Frances Chan
Photo Researcher: Jamshed Mistry

Photographs by: Big Stock Photo (p. 5); **Digital Vision** (background, pp. 12–13); **Getty Images**
(Tuaregs at fireside, p. 13; background, pp. 16–17; Maasai herders, p. 16; background,
pp. 20–21; woman with baby on back, p. 20; boys dancing, p. 21; injection, woman carrying
water, p. 23; background, pp. 24–25; gorilla protest, p. 27; cacao picker, p. 28; woman
and child in fields, p. 28; gorilla tourism, p. 29; p. 31; African shanty town, pp. 32–33);
Jennifer and Brian Lupton (teenagers, pp. 32–33); © **Jonathan Reid/Images of Africa** (p. 30);
Photolibrary (cover; Tuareg well, p. 13; canoe, p. 15; Maasai family, fenced village, p. 16;
cooking, classroom, p. 17; background, pp. 28–29; village, p. 28; market day, orphaned gorillas,
p. 29); © **Randy Olson/National Geographic Image Collection** (p. 18); **Reuters** (salt caravan,
p. 11); **Tranz: Corbis** (p. 3; pp. 7–9; Nairobi cityscape, shanty town, p. 11; Theodore Roosevelt,
p. 15; Maasai craft stall, safari driver, p. 17; p.19; Mbuti village, men by fire, p. 20; Mbuti hunt,
okapi, p. 21; p. 22; Dian Fossey, p. 27); © **Victor Englebert** (p. 12; bathing baby, Tuaregs with
camels, p. 13; inset photos, pp. 24–25); **Courtesy of www.hipporoller.org** (woman with water
roller, p. 23)

All illustrations and other photographs © Weldon Owen Education Inc.

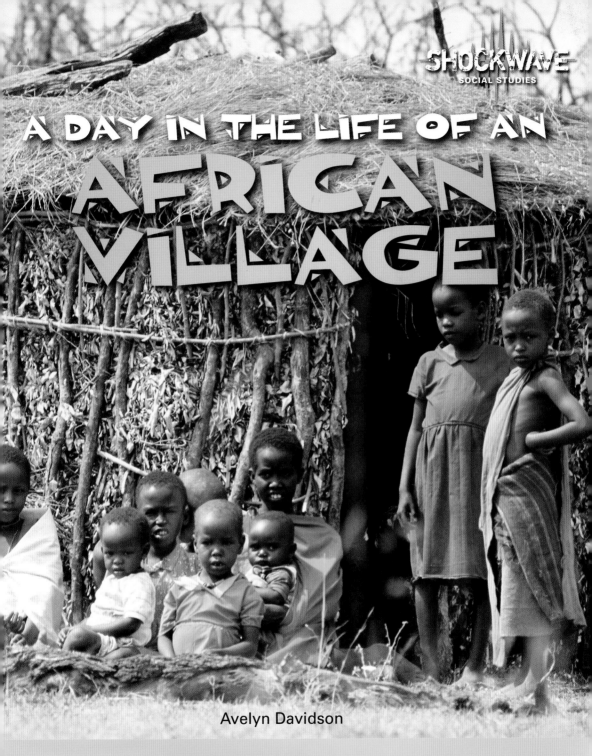

SHOCKWAVE
SOCIAL STUDIES

A DAY IN THE LIFE OF AN
AFRICAN VILLAGE

Avelyn Davidson

children's press®

An imprint of Scholastic Inc.
NEW YORK • TORONTO • LONDON • AUCKLAND • SYDNEY
MEXICO CITY • NEW DELHI • HONG KONG
DANBURY, CONNECTICUT

CHECK THESE OUT!

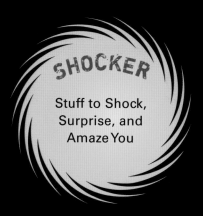

SHOCKER

Stuff to Shock,
Surprise, and
Amaze You

Quick Recaps
and Notable
Notes

Word Stunners
and Other Oddities

The Heads-Up
on Expert Reading

Links to More
Information

CONTENTS

colony (*KOL uh nee*) a settlement under the rule
of a parent country

continent one of the seven main land masses on the earth

culture the lifestyle, traditions, and beliefs of a group of people

deforestation the permanent removal of the trees in a forest

desertification the process of becoming arid and lacking
in vegetation, like a desert

endangered close to becoming one of the last of its kind
left on the earth

ethnic having to do with a group of people who share
the same national origins, language, or culture

tribal having to do with a group of people who share
the same ancestors, customs, and laws

For additional vocabulary, see Glossary on page 34.

The word *colony* comes
from the Latin *colonia*,
meaning "settled land."
Related words include:
colonize and *colonial*.

This Maasai woman is wearing a colorful beaded necklace. The color red symbolizes the tribe, and is believed to frighten lions.

To many people, the image of Africa is people in villages living in harmony with nature. Even today, most Africans live in small **rural** villages. For hundreds or even thousands of years, the many African **cultures** have maintained their own **customs**. **Tribal** and **ethnic** groups use traditional farming, hunting, and herding techniques suited for the varied settings – desert or jungle, mountain or savanna – in which they live.

About 900 million people live on this vast **continent**. Every year, millions of Africans move from their villages into cities. Some of them are seeking a modern life.

Others have been forced from their villages by famine or war. Often these refugees struggle to retain their **diverse** traditions of artwork, child-rearing, and storytelling.

So far, the modernization of Africa seems to have caused more harm than good. No one village is typical of Africa. But all rural Africans are challenged to find ways to maintain their traditions. They must find new ways that will allow them to **integrate** their communities with the modern world.

Facts About Africa

- Population: 900 million. Expected to double by the middle of this century.

- Percentage of population aged under 21 years of age: 71 percent

- Most populous city: Lagos, Nigeria, with 16.9 million people

- Number of languages spoken: more than 2,000

- Number of refugees **displaced** by war and conflict: 15 million

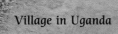

Village in Uganda

AFRICAN SNAPSHOT

Africa is the earth's second largest continent. It is made up of 53 independent countries. About two thousand different languages are spoken there. Africa's landscapes and climates are more diverse than those of any other continent. There are deserts, mountains, plains, and forests.

The climate in central and western Africa is lush and **tropical**. In the north and south of this region, there is a narrow **temperate** zone. Fertile croplands in Nigeria and rich **volcanic** soils in much of eastern Africa produce crops that feed hundreds of millions of people. But deserts, rain forests, and drought-plagued areas can only support a limited human population. Climate change is also displacing millions of people.

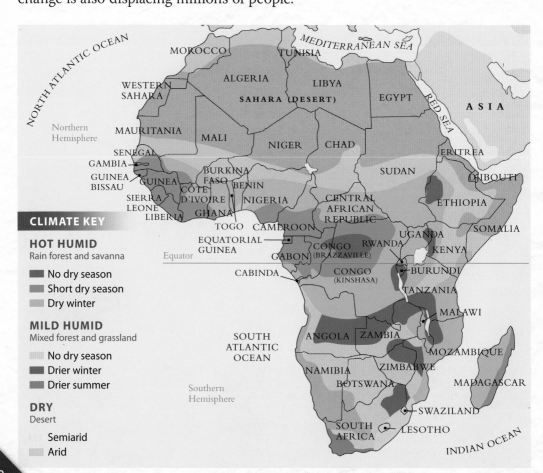

NORTH ATLANTIC OCEAN

MEDITERRANEAN SEA

MOROCCO TUNISIA

ALGERIA LIBYA
WESTERN
SAHARA
SAHARA (DESERT) EGYPT
ASIA

RED SEA

Northern
Hemisphere MAURITANIA
MALI NIGER CHAD ERITREA
SENEGAL
GAMBIA
GUINEA GUINEA BURKINA SUDAN DJIBOUTI
BISSAU FASO BENIN
COTE
SIERRA D'IVOIRE NIGERIA CENTRAL ETHIOPIA
LEONE AFRICAN
LIBERIA GHANA REPUBLIC
TOGO CAMEROON SOMALIA

CLIMATE KEY

EQUATORIAL UGANDA
GUINEA CONGO RWANDA KENYA
HOT HUMID Equator (BRAZZAVILLE)
Rain forest and savanna GABON BURUNDI
CABINDA CONGO
- No dry season (KINSHASA) TANZANIA
- Short dry season MALAWI
- Dry winter

MILD HUMID
Mixed forest and grassland SOUTH ANGOLA ZAMBIA
ATLANTIC MOZAMBIQUE
- No dry season OCEAN ZIMBABWE
- Drier winter NAMIBIA MADAGASCAR
- Drier summer Southern BOTSWANA
Hemisphere
SWAZILAND
DRY
Desert SOUTH LESOTHO
- Semiarid AFRICA
- Arid INDIAN OCEAN

Salt caravan crossing the Sahara desert

More Africans than ever before live in cities. Almost three million people live in Nairobi, the capital of Kenya (shown below). Nairobi is nicknamed "The Green City in the Sun." It is famous for its skyline and parklands. However, half of its population live in crowded slums.

A TUAREG CAMP

The Sahara is the world's largest desert. The Tuareg people have lived a **nomadic** life in the Sahara for thousands of years. They are known as the "Blue Men" for their indigo blue clothing. Traditionally, the Tuareg have operated the camel caravans connecting North Africa to the cities in the south. Today, most Tuareg live in villages of about 30 to 100 people. These Tuareg raise livestock or work as farmers.

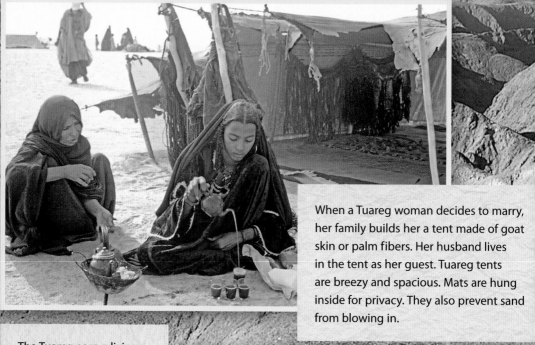

When a Tuareg woman decides to marry, her family builds her a tent made of goat skin or palm fibers. Her husband lives in the tent as her guest. Tuareg tents are breezy and spacious. Mats are hung inside for privacy. They also prevent sand from blowing in.

The Tuareg earn a living selling camels. In return they buy **millet**, sugar, and tea. They also grow crops, including barley and corn, and raise goats, cattle, and chickens. Long, woolen robes and head coverings protect the Tuareg from the fierce sun and chilly nights of the Sahara.

At nighttime, families gather to tell stories and play music. Popular stories tell of jinns, or spirits, who play tricks on desert travelers.

Water is scarce in the desert. The Tuareg build wells where they find an oasis. They carry the water back to their villages. Not a drop of water goes to waste.

Villages are often relocated. It takes only about two hours to pack up the family tent. The tents are tied to the backs of camels for transporting to a new place.

A TURBULENT HISTORY

The continent of Africa has had a long and turbulent history. Beginning in the sixteenth century, slave traders captured Africans from many parts of Africa. They took them to the Caribbean islands and to North America, where they were sold as plantation slaves.

Early European traders and explorers returned from Africa with stories of gold and jewels. They also took back African fruits and spices. Soon, several European countries were claiming parts of Africa as **colonies**.

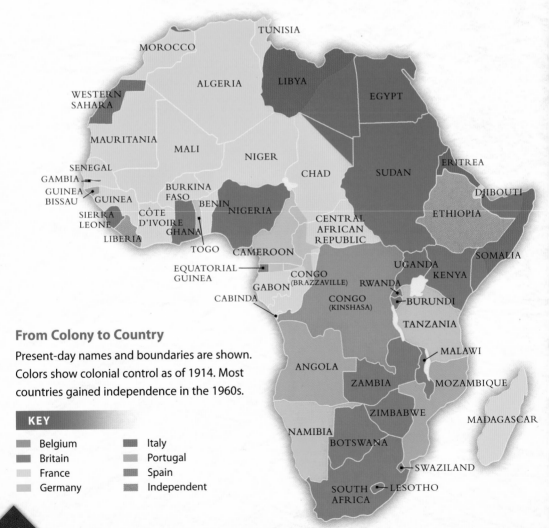

From Colony to Country

Present-day names and boundaries are shown. Colors show colonial control as of 1914. Most countries gained independence in the 1960s.

KEY

Belgium	Italy
Britain	Portugal
France	Spain
Germany	Independent

Most historians now agree that colonization harmed the African people. European governors often created artificial racial divisions within local tribes. Some of these divisions still cause fighting today. Ivory merchants and other traders enslaved the people in some colonies, particularly the Congo. They tried to **convert** Africans to Christian religions.

Some entire colonies were put to work growing a single crop, such as coffee. A single bad growing season or drop in prices could devastate millions of people. Even in well-run colonies, Africans were not allowed to govern themselves. When countries became independent, their new leaders had no experience of self-government on which to rely.

SHOCKER

In 1909, U.S. President Theodore Roosevelt went to Africa. He wanted to get a collection of wildlife trophies for the Smithsonian Institution. Thousands of animals were killed on his expedition.

Theodore Roosevelt poses with an elephant he has shot.

Colonization

- created racial divisions
- enslaved many people
- left little room for self-government
- stripped valuable resources

In the nineteenth century, Europeans searched for the source of the Nile and Congo rivers. On their difficult journeys upriver, the explorers sometimes clashed with local tribes. Africans were relied upon to carry boats around waterfalls and other obstacles. This photo shows Mary Kingsley, a British explorer who traveled to Africa in the 1890s. She was not afraid to venture into unmapped areas. Kingsley also acted as a doctor in the villages she visited.

A MAASAI VILLAGE

The Maasai are a seminomadic people who live in parts of Kenya and Tanzania. They follow the seasons in search of grass and water for their livestock. Maasai determine their wealth by the amount of livestock they own. Cows are their most important animals. According to the Maasai religion, god gave every cow in the world to the Maasai. The Maasai often greet each other by asking, "How are your cows?"

Traditionally, the Maasai were warriors and hunters. Some people still believe that lions are frightened by the sight of a Maasai man wearing his bright red *shuka*, or robe.

The Maasai herd their cattle and goats on the plains. This is becoming more difficult for them to do as the open plains disappear. Much of the plains are now set aside as wildlife preserves.

Men tie thorny branches together to form a fence around the village. The sharp thorns protect the Maasai and their animals from wildlife.

The Maasai live in huts that take about seven months to build. First the women weave a framework out of branches. Then they cover the structure with sundried plaster. Layers of dried grass on the roof keep the hut cool inside.

The Maasai eat the meat and drink the milk from their cows. On special occasions, they drink cow's blood. Today, the Maasai also eat cornmeal, potatoes, and cabbage.

The Maasai are famous for their artwork. They decorate bracelets, necklaces, and shields with colorful beads.

The Maasai must pay to send their children to schools like this one. Many young people leave their villages to attend school in cities, such as Nairobi. Other children are educated in the traditional way, by their elders.

I get it! It looks like the spreads in this book alternate between information about Africa and different villages. Knowing what to expect makes reading easier.

Today, many Maasai villages earn money from tourism. The men drive or guide visitors in the game preserves.

17

HARDSHIP AND WAR

The African continent has billions of dollars worth of oil, gold, diamonds, and other natural resources. Many international corporations have profited from this wealth. Few Africans have benefited. Instead, **dictators** and armies have fought to control their countries' mines and oilfields.

Some of the worst fighting has occurred in the Congo, a diamond-rich region in central Africa. From 1996 to 2003, eight countries and dozens of other armed groups fought for control of the country. More than three million people were killed. A similar number of people lost their homes.

Toleka traders trudge with their bicycles along paths in the forest. Their bikes are piled high with cookware, shoes, food, fuel, armaments, and clothing. They sell these items in return for timber, gold, and wild animals.

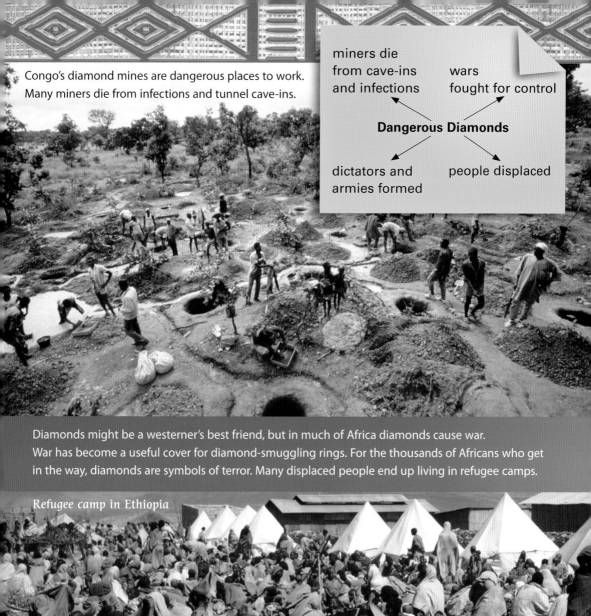

Congo's diamond mines are dangerous places to work. Many miners die from infections and tunnel cave-ins.

miners die from cave-ins and infections

wars fought for control

Dangerous Diamonds

dictators and armies formed

people displaced

Diamonds might be a westerner's best friend, but in much of Africa diamonds cause war. War has become a useful cover for diamond-smuggling rings. For the thousands of Africans who get in the way, diamonds are symbols of terror. Many displaced people end up living in refugee camps.

Refugee camp in Ethiopia

SHOCKER

People made homeless by war may end up in refugee camps like this one. These camps often lack food and clean water, and are vulnerable to attackers.

A MBUTI HUNTING CAMP

The Mbuti pygmies live in the remote Ituri forests in the Congo. According to the Mbuti, the forest is a spirit that keeps them from harm. Bad things can happen only when the forest is asleep. The Mbuti sing songs to awaken the forest They ask the forest for its protection. The Mbuti believe that *indura nee bokbu*, "the forest is everything."

However, **deforestation** is threatening the Ituri forests. Timber and mining companies are cutting down thousands of trees. **Poachers** are hunting the wildlife the Mbuti depend on.

The Mbuti organize their *endu*, or shelters, to avoid conflict. Friends live closer together, while enemies are kept apart. Each year, these camps are abandoned as groups of hunters search the forest for honey.

The Mbuti gather to tell jokes and stories.

Mbuti mothers sing to their children even before they are born. On hunting trips, the women carry their babies in slings.

Mbuti children are grouped by age and educated in the village. These groups last for life. The members call each other *amua'i* (sister) or *apua'i* (brother).

The Mbuti hunt with long nets like this one. The women form large circles in the forest. Then they drive antelopes, monkeys, and other animals toward the men standing in the center. The men trap the animals and kill them with their spears.

The Mbuti share the forest with the okapi, or forest giraffe. The okapi is found only in the Congo. Scientists are working to save the okapi and their shrinking habitat.

CHALLENGE AND CHANGE

Many African countries are struggling with serious problems. Some governments are weakened by violence, **corruption**, and debts to western countries. AIDS kills more than two million Africans every year. As the rate of desertification increases, traditional cultures are forced to modernize, or suffer famines. Overcrowded cities often lack enough clean drinking water.

However, important progress is being made. In Botswana, diamond profits are used to provide free education and medicine for the poor. Many people are working to combat causes of desertification. Forests are being planted in vulnerable areas to protect the land from overuse.

Zamo (center) is living with AIDS. He is traveling to a World AIDS Day event to speak about his experiences. Zamo is on an HIV-treatment program that helps AIDS victims from underserved areas.

The water roller is a clever invention that has helped many African people. Women fill drums with water and wheel them back to the village instead of having to carry cans and buckets on their heads.

Millions of Africans die each year as a result of water shortages. More than half of rural Africans are forced to drink unclean water. This can cause parasitic infections and other deadly illnesses. Industrial pollution and expanding cities have reduced the amount of water available for farming. Many African villages are also threatened by climate changes. These changes are disrupting yearly rainfall patterns. Severe droughts can permanently ruin farmland and cause famines.

A blood sample is taken to see whether this girl has the virus that causes AIDS.

Life in Africa

Negatives	Positives
• violence/corruption	• access to free education
• AIDS	• improved medical and rural facilities
• desertification	
• overcrowded cities	• forests being planted

23

A VILLAGE IN GHANA

More than forty different languages are spoken in Ghana. Millions of people live in Accra, the capital, and in other areas along the coast. Traders sell gold, diamonds, timber, and cacao to foreign companies. This has made Ghana the richest country in West Africa.

In the interior of Ghana, different ethnic groups live traditional lives in small villages. One group is called the Ashanti. They make up about 14 percent of Ghana's population. The Ashanti believe that all plants and animals have souls. They worship their ancestors. They celebrate marriage, birth, and other occasions with colorful ceremonies. The men and women wear colorful *kente* cloth, play drums, and feast.

The Ashanti live in extended families. The elders elect a "house father," or leader. Usually the eldest brother in the family is chosen.

The village grows bananas and oranges. These are sold in the markets.

Cacao is an important crop. The cacao beans are dried on a table in the sun. Then the cacao is sold or traded for food. This cacao will be sold to a Fair Trade company.

These women have a sewing business. They make bright clothes to sell in the markets. The money is going toward a well for their village. The village wants its own source of clean water.

Without a well, the women in this village have to walk three miles to the river every day to fetch water. They must boil the water before drinking it.

Many Africans sell cacao and other products to Fair Trade organizations. These organizations agree to buy goods for a price that allows the seller to earn a decent living. The buyers often help workers expand their businesses. They make sure no one forces them to work in unsafe conditions. Certified Fair Trade products are often marked with a special label (right).

FAIRTRADE

Million is a strange word. It comes from the Latin *mille*, meaning "thousand." But a million is actually a thousand thousand. Examples where *milli* means a thousandth include: *millimeter*, *millisecond*, and *milliliter*.

DID YOU KNOW?

The Ashanti once ruled a large kingdom in western Africa. They grew rich trading gold and *kente* to Europeans. In 1900, after four wars against Great Britain, the kingdom finally fell to the English. The English forces were strengthened by help from Nigerian troops.

25

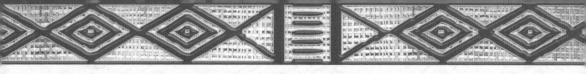

ANiMALS AT RiSK

Africa is home to the most spectacular wildlife on earth. Lions, wildebeest, and cheetahs are some of the animals that roam the plains. Fierce hippos and crocodiles live along tropical riverbanks. Rain forests are home to gorillas, bonobos, and other rare **primates**. But in many places in Africa, people and wild animals are in conflict. Forests are burned to create new farmlands. Starving predators who have lost their habitat are often forced to prey on livestock, or even people.

Poachers are sometimes the most serious threat to **endangered** animals. Armed guards patrol many wildlife preserves in Africa. Some are instructed to shoot poachers when they find them. Still, many poachers feel they cannot survive without eating or selling protected animals. They worry that they will starve when all the wild animals are gone.

One solution is **ecotourism**. Many former poachers now put their skills to work as guides in wildlife preserves. This peaceful work offers a future for both animals and rural Africans.

Can you name these endangered African species?

Endangered Animal
1. Rhinoceros
2. Mandrill
3. Leopard
4. Giraffe
5. Gray parrot
6. Sable antelope
7. Chimpanzee
8. Lion
9. Mountain gorilla
10. Elephant
11. Bongo
12. Cheetah
13. Spotted hyena
14. Okapi

Villagers make posters of baby gorillas orphaned by war or poaching. People from overseas can choose a gorilla to adopt and **sponsor**. The money goes to the village to support the babies.

Great! I already know something about endangered African animals from programs on TV. Noticing these types of connections makes reading much more interesting.

Dian Fossey, an American zoologist, let the world know of the plight of mountain gorillas. These intelligent primates are often snared in nets like those pictured here. Fossey hired locals for anti-poaching patrols. She was killed in 1985, possibly by a poacher. Her murder remains unsolved.

A VILLAGE IN RWANDA

Rwanda is Africa's most densely populated country. It is also one of the most fertile. The fields are terraced. Not a scrap of land is unused. Shortage of land has caused people to push into the protected forests. This has endangered the mountain gorilla. Now, in many villages, **conservationists** and villagers work together to protect the animals. Students learn about conservation programs. Young people are trained as tour guides and conservationists. Villagers are learning to live with the wild animals. They are learning that this can help provide them with a better future.

Everyone shares the work in the fields.

Ninety percent of people in Rwanda live in small villages. They are farmers. A patchwork of crops covers nearly every inch of the volcanic soil.

Many villages grow tea and cacao. These crops provide Rwanda with export revenue.

On market day, villagers trade crops.

Many villagers work in conservation. They care for baby gorillas orphaned through war or poaching.

Gorilla ecotourism is becoming a big source of revenue for many villages. Guides take tourists into the forests to view the gorillas.

The *en-* prefix in words such as *endanger* means "to cause to be," or "to make." Other examples include: *encase* (put in a case); *enable* (make able); and *encircle* (put in a circle).

AFRICA'S FUTURE

Humans have lived in Africa for more than seven million years, longer than anywhere else on the earth. Great empires once ruled along the border of the Sahara, in the Congo region, and in other areas of the continent, including Egypt in the northeast. Many tribes grew rich by trading with Arab and European merchants.

In the nineteenth century, most of Africa was conquered by England, Germany, and other European countries. The natural resources and native populations of the continent were **exploited** for the benefit of these colonizing powers. One colony, the Congo, was actually considered the personal property of King Leopold II of Belgium!

The African people began to regain their independence in 1956. But many countries still struggle with poverty, violence, and illness. Fortunately, Africa is a land with many resources, including oil, diamonds, gold, and spectacular wildlife preserves. Most of all, Africa is rich with many cultures and traditions, both old and new.

Wildlife preserve, Malawi

Wangari Maathai is a Maasai woman who has won the **Nobel Peace Prize**. In 1977, she began a tree-planting campaign in Kenya to reforest the land. Her organization also develops tree nurseries and provides jobs for rural people. "The solutions to our problems lie within us," says Wangari Maathai. "No matter what problems we face, we can still protect the environment and think of future generations."

31

African countries owe more than $200 billion in debts. Over the years, corrupt African dictatorships have borrowed money from the United States and European countries for their own personal gain. This money has not benefited the African people. Today, most people in Africa live on less than $2 per day, but African countries are forced to spend $14 billion a year paying off old debts.

WHAT DO YOU THINK?

Should wealthy countries cancel all of Africa's debts?

PRO

Many of the governments that took out these debts aren't even in power anymore. It's not fair to punish people for the mistakes of others. African countries should be allowed to forget the debt and start again.

African governments need to spend their money on reducing poverty, modernizing industry, and improving health care. In 2005, a group of eight of the wealthiest countries announced that they would cancel some of the debt owed by the world's poorest countries, many of which are in Africa. Some people believe that it would be fairer to cancel the whole debt because rich countries have exploited Africa for hundreds of years.

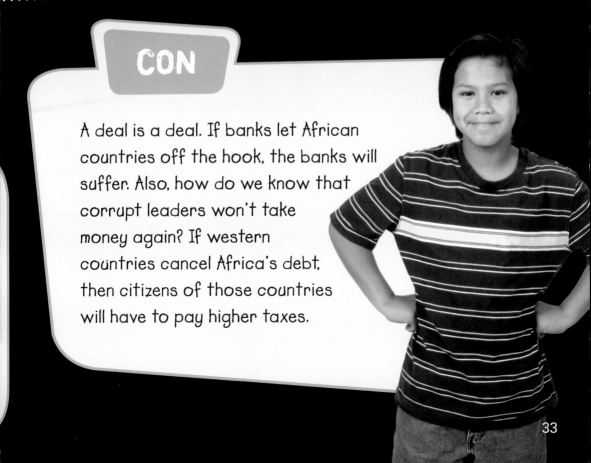

CON

A deal is a deal. If banks let African countries off the hook, the banks will suffer. Also, how do we know that corrupt leaders won't take money again? If western countries cancel Africa's debt, then citizens of those countries will have to pay higher taxes.

GLOSSARY

conservationist a person who works to protect wild plants and animals and their environments

convert (*con VERT*) to get a person to change his or her beliefs, religion, or the way he or she lives

corruption the act of being dishonest and unlawful

custom a practice followed by people of a particular group

dictator someone who has complete control of a country, often ruling unjustly

displace to move someone or something from its usual place

diverse varied, of different types

ecotourism (*ee koh TOOR iz uhm*) tourist activities based on respect for nature

exploit (*eks PLOIT*) to take advantage of someone or something

integrate to combine several things or people into one whole

millet a grass-like wheat that is raised for its small, edible seeds

Nobel Peace Prize a prize awarded annually to a person who has made great achievements in bringing about world peace

nomadic moving from place to place

poacher a person who illegally kills or captures protected animals

primate an order of mammals that includes humans, monkeys, apes, and lemurs

rural having to do with the countryside; not urban

semiarid having very low annual rainfall, but able to support some grassland and vegetation

sponsor to pay money to support a good cause

Primate

temperate having warm summers and cold winters

tropical related to the hot areas of the earth near the equator

volcanic produced by, discharged from, or having to do with a volcano

FIND OUT MORE

BOOKS

Ayo, Yvonne. *Africa*. DK Eyewitness, 2000.

King, David C. *Rwanda*. Marshall Cavendish Benchmark, 2007.

McQuail, Lisa. *The Masai of Africa*. Lerner Publishing Group, 2001.

Pierre, Yvette La. *Ghana in Pictures*. Lerner Publishing Group, 2004.

Reynolds, Jan. *Sahara*. Lee & Low Books, 2007.

Strom, Laura Layton. *Caught With a Catch: Poaching in Africa*. Scholastic Inc., 2008.

Willis, Terri. *Democratic Republic of the Congo*. Children's Press, 2004.

WEB SITES

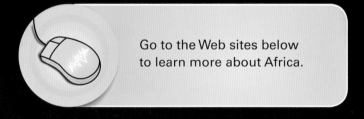

Go to the Web sites below to learn more about Africa.

www.oxfam.org.uk/coolplanet/kidsweb/children.htm

www.bornfree.org.uk

www.pbskids.org/africa

http://news.bbc.co.uk/cbbcnews/hi/find_out/guides/2003/ life_for_african_kids/newsid_2686000/2686903.stm

INDEX

ABOUT THE AUTHOR

Avelyn Davidson is the author of many fiction and nonfiction books for children. Avelyn loves to travel the world, and has been to many countries in Africa. She's seen wild animals on safari and many stunning natural landscapes. Avelyn was touched by the wonderful people that she met in Africa – in bustling towns and small villages. She hopes that her book will encourage people to visit this diverse and colorful continent.